Upper Floor

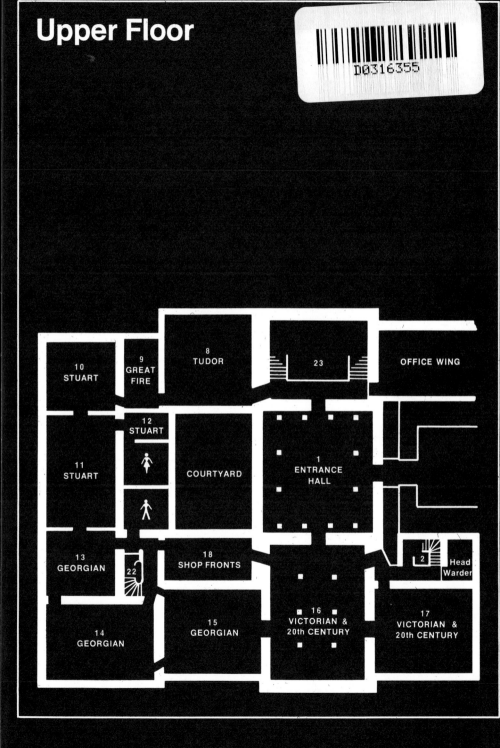

Guide to the London Museum

London Her Majesty's Stationery Office 1972

Frontispiece

Kensington Palace, with the gardens designed by
Henry Wise for Queen Anne. Engraving *c.* 1710–20.

© Crown copyright 1972

First published 1960
Second edition 1972

SBN 11 290114 X

Printed in England for Her Majesty's Stationery
Office by W. S. Cowell Ltd, Ipswich
Dd 500601 K320

Preface

The London Museum was founded in 1911 by the 2nd Viscount Esher and the 1st Viscount Harcourt, with the active support of King George V and Queen Mary, and was opened to the public in the State Apartments of Kensington Palace on 8 April 1912. In 1913 it became a National Museum under Treasury control, and the collections were vested in a Board of Trustees. The following summer it moved to Lancaster House, the lease of which had been given to the nation by Lord Leverhulme primarily for the use of the Museum but also for purposes of official entertainment. There it remained for twenty-five years. During the Second World War the Museum was closed, and in 1945 Lancaster House, which had been one of the most glittering of town mansions in the 19th century and was uniquely suited to entertainment on the grand scale, was taken over for government hospitality. Negotiations were then started for the acquisition of land for a new building. These concentrated on various sites on the South Bank, though Holland Park was also considered. Meanwhile, the Museum was granted a lease of premises in Kensington Palace by King George VI, and opened here in 1951.

In 1960 a scheme was evolved to merge the existing London Museum and the Guildhall Museum into a new comprehensive museum of the history of London, to be called the Museum of London. The necessary Act of Parliament was passed in 1965, and provided for the allocation of a site within the City by the City Corporation, that the Museum should receive financial support by means of equal contributions from the Government, the City Corporation and the London County Council (now the G.L.C), and that the Museum should be administered by an independent Board of Governors appointed in equal proportions by the three contributing authorities. Powell &

Moya were appointed architects, and building was begun on the new site at the south-west corner of Barbican in April 1971.

The present Guide, which is designed to meet the needs of the public during our last years at Kensington, is intended rather as an indication of the Museum's purpose – the illustration of the history of London – and of the range of its collections, than as a room-to-room guide, since, in the years immediately ahead, experimental displays and exhibitions connected with work on designing the display area in the Museum of London may interrupt some of the present arrangements. I hope for your indulgence, interest and support. We in turn will endeavour to make of the new Museum of London something entirely original in museum design, a layout which, evolving from the nature of the subject-matter rather than from accepted theories and coming firmly into the 20th century, will offer the visitor not just the familiar miscellaneous collection of by-gones, but meaningful relationships between objects and life as it was once lived, a vivid and imaginative sequence of spaces encompassing the whole development and culture of London and the manifold ways in which Londoners have spent and enjoyed their lives. The demise of the old London Museum will not be a moment of sadness but the signal for new intellectual and visual adventures, and for a wholly new service to the public.

John Hayes
Director
Kensington Palace.

1 Queen Victoria's First Council, 20 June 1837,
by Sir David Wilkie. The setting was the present
entrance hall of the Museum. (By gracious
permission of H.M. The Queen.)

Kensington Palace

In 1689 King William III bought a small Jacobean house (Nottingham House, Kensington) in a healthy part of the environs, away from the centre of London. This was converted and enlarged by Sir Christopher Wren, and renamed Kensington House. Further substantial alterations were carried out later for William III (the King's Gallery was added in 1695–6); and the centre of the palace was rebuilt in the Palladian style for George I. The rooms occupied by the Museum were converted into apartments for Edward, Duke of Kent in the first decade of the 19th century, and his daughter, the future Queen Victoria, was born in the room in the north-east corner in 1819. Visitors will notice that the elegant Regency detailing in the door-surrounds and other features survives throughout. The splendid staircase, which is hung with pictures, was originally the grand approach to the Duke's apartments from an entrance hall (now the Royal Costume room) and a portico in Clock Court. The lower floor was occupied by kitchens and other services. Kensington Palace is rich in royal associations: it was the favoured residence of William III, Queen Anne and the first two Georges, Queen Victoria lived here with her mother before she came to the throne (Fig. 1), in the suite in the State Apartments now devoted to her memory, and Queen Mary was born here in 1867.

1a The carved hood bearing the monogram of William and Mary, which surmounts the public entrance to the State Apartments.

1b The King's Staircase, as decorated by William Kent for George I. The wrought ironwork is by Jean Tijou.

Prehistoric

Britain was not the most inviting place for early prehistoric man, as the thick woodland and marsh which covered the lowland areas of the country (Fig. 3) made habitation almost impossible. But during the hundreds of thousands of years of the Ice Age which preceded the warmer conditions in which trees could flourish, the melt-water from the glaciers had deposited extensive layers or terraces of gravel in the valley floors, and this light well-drained soil made settlement feasible in certain places along the Thames: indeed, the distribution of the terraces has strongly influenced development in London up to the 19th century. Flint hand axes and other implements belonging to hunters of the Ice Age period, of which the Museum has an outstanding collection, have been found in the gravel beds of the London region.

Successive waves of nomadic immigrants from north-eastern Europe in the 10,000 years or so which intervened between the recession of the ice and the coming of the Romans, have settled along the Thames. Up to about 2000 B.C. most of these people made their livelihood from fishing and trading as well as from hunting: some of the harpoons they used are exhibited. The people of the Middle Stone Age were the first to attempt to cut down the trees, and the flint axes which they developed (now known as 'Thames Picks') seem to have been used for this purpose. It was not until towards 2000 B.C. that settlers of the New Stone Age introduced a new type of economy based on agriculture, growing their own food and raising livestock: these people were also capable of a primitive kind of pottery and many examples (Fig. 2) have been excavated, notably in the vicinity of Hammersmith and Mortlake, which seems to have been their main centre of settlement in the London area. Fresh settlers, from the Low Countries and Germany, arrived in the Thames valley during the Bronze Age. Their

2 Bowl from a Neolithic rubbish pit at Heathrow.

4

3 The site of London in prehistoric times. This reconstruction drawing by Forestier shows the wide marshes bordering the Thames, cut on the north bank by the Fleet and Walbrook rivers.

4 Neolithic jadeite axe from the Thames at Mortlake.

most important settlement was evidently at
Brentford, as extensive finds of bronze
implements have been made there, including
numerous examples of the characteristic late
Bronze Age leaf-shaped swords. Cremation of
the dead was introduced at this time, and
pottery urns excavated from cemeteries in
west Middlesex are on display.

There were three main phases of colonisation
in the Iron Age, the 1000 years prior to the
Roman invasion. The village at Heathrow
(Fig. 6), where successive excavations have
been carried out during the development of the
airport, was a settlement of the first phase,
which started about 500 B.C. Early Celtic art
was introduced to Britain during the second
phase, from around 300 B.C., the best examples
in the Museum being the bronze chariot hand-
grip found at Brentford and the horse-bit
from Walthamstow (Fig. 7). The Belgae,
tribesmen from northern France and Belgium,
were the colonisers of the third phase. They
were the people we now call the ancient
Britons. They set up kingdoms in different
parts of south-east England and organised
powerful resistance to the Roman legions after
the arrival of Claudius in A.D. 43. It was the
legendary Boudicca (Boadicea), Queen of the
Iceni, who commanded the tribesmen from
East Anglia in the revolt which led to the
destruction of the first Roman city of London
in A.D. 61. Though, in common with their
predecessors, some of the Belgae settled along
the banks of the Thames, there is no evidence
to indicate any large-scale settlement in the
London area which could be construed as a
predecessor of the Roman city. London was
the creation of the Romans, and it was
founded where it was because the invaders
needed a base with the facilities of a port and
with communications on both sides of the
river: the site of London was the point nearest
to the estuary where the Thames was still tidal
(and therefore navigable) that it was possible
to build a bridge.

5 Bronze spearhead,
c. 1000–900 B.C., found
in the Thames at
Brentford.

6 The Iron Age temple and village at Heathrow,
c. 500–300 B.C., excavated in 1944, as reconstructed
by Alan Sorrell.

7 Three-linked Iron Age snaffle-bit from
Walthamstow, *c.* 300 B.C.

Roman

The Romans constructed their bridge across
the Thames a little to the east of the present
London Bridge, and the town grew up around
the bridgehead on the northern shore,
extending in the direction of the easterly of the
two hills, Cornhill, where the forum or
market-place was established. The streets
were laid out in the symmetrical fashion
customary in Roman town-planning, and
arterial roads fanned out in the direction of
Silchester (between Reading and Basingstoke),
Verulamium (St. Albans) and Camulodunum
(Colchester), the capital of the province.

After the sack of A.D. 61, London replaced
Colchester as the Roman capital and the city
was totally replanned. A vast basilica or town-
hall was constructed adjoining the forum, and
the governor's palace was built on the
riverfront: its remains have recently been
discovered during building operations near
Cannon Street Station. No traces of an
amphitheatre have ever been found. Towards
the end of the 1st century a sizeable stone fort
(the Cripplegate Fort) was built to the
north-west of the city to house the garrison
normally attached to any Roman capital. The
defensive walls which, contrary to general
belief, seem not to have been continued along
the river-bank, were constructed a century or
more later: parts of them are visible on Tower
Hill and in St. Alphage's churchyard. Though
the area within the walls, about 330 acres, was
never wholly developed, settlement soon
spread onto the western hill (Ludgate Hill),
and in the late 2nd century the marshy area
between Cornhill and St. Paul's, where up to
then a market had flourished along the banks
of the Walbrook, was reclaimed and became a
fashionable residential district. A number of
industries, of which leather-working was
certainly one, grew up here, and an impressive
Mithraic temple served this neighbourhood:
some of the sculptures which belonged to the

8 Late 1st-century jug of buff earthenware, found
in Southwark, inscribed *LONDINI AD FANUM
ISIDIS* or *London, at the shrine of Isis.*

9 London, *c.* 200 A.D., as reconstructed by Alan Sorrell. The walled area is dominated by the Forum and by the Cripplegate Fort in the north-west corner.

10 Red-glazed bowl, decorated with a hunting scene. Made at Lezoux in Gaul, *c.* 70–120 A.D.

11 Roman iron tools, all found in London: a saw, a borer fitted with leather washers to form a grip and an awl stamped with the maker's name *TITULI*.

12 Statue of a river god from the Walbrook, a sculpture originally in the Mithraic Temple.

13 Bronze coin minted in London, *c.* 306 A.D., to commemorate the Emperor Constantius. The mintmark of London is the letters *PLN* below the altar.

temple are in the Museum (Fig. 12), but the more important examples from the 1954 excavations are in the Guildhall Museum. There must have been many fine houses and public buildings in London, from which mosaics and examples of wall decoration have survived, but wattle and daub construction continued to be the norm for the houses of poorer people; the hut-villages in the environs, as evidence from Brentford shows, cannot have differed much from the characteristic Iron Age settlements.

London's commercial activity had been considerable even before the sack of Boudicca, and over the following two hundred years the port developed into one of the most flourishing entrepôts in the Empire. Little archaeological evidence has been found as to the nature of the wharves and warehouses, but a substantial part of a Roman ship, dating from the end of the 3rd century or later, was found in 1910 on the site of County Hall, and is preserved in the Museum. Amongst the most common imports, well represented in the collections, were the Gaulish red-glazed pots, bowls (Fig. 10) and dishes (mistakenly called Samian ware) and the amphorae, or two-handled jars, which were used as containers for wine and oil. Perhaps the best-known piece of London pottery is the jug found in Southwark (Fig. 8) which bears an inscription recording the presence of a temple to the Egyptian god Isis in this vicinity. Native industries included bronze-, enamel- and glass-working, and innumerable domestic and personal articles, of which oil-lamps, candlesticks, keys, brooches and finger-rings are especially common, testify to the high degree of material culture which Roman London enjoyed. By the end of the 3rd century there was a mint active in London (Fig. 13), but it very soon ceased to strike gold or silver, and in the course of this same century the progressive collapse of the Roman Empire brought about by the pressure of barbarian invasion gradually reduced the extent of London's overseas trade, and prosperity declined. In the early 4th century came the first of the Saxon invasions, and finally, in A.D. 410, when Rome itself was threatened by the Goths, the Romans left Britain to its fate.

Saxon
and Viking

Though London in early Saxon times was probably not a town of squatters among half-ruined buildings, as has often been thought, its importance as an administrative and commercial centre must have dwindled to nothing, since the Saxons were a farming people, settling in communities along the banks of the Thames much as their predecessors had done in the Iron Age. Some pottery and loomweights from such a settlement were found on the site of the Savoy. By the beginning of the 7th century, however, London had become the chief town of the East Saxons, and site of a bishopric; a church dedicated to St. Paul was built on the highest ground in the city, and settlement spread gradually eastwards, following the opposite course to the development of Roman London.

By the 8th century, as we know from the writings of Bede, London was once again enjoying an extensive overseas trade, but the succeeding two centuries were darkened by repeated attacks from first the Vikings and then the Danes. London, whose bridge, strengthened under Alfred with parapets and towers, impeded the passage of the Viking fleets, became a centre of national resistance; and the Museum contains a splendid group of axes (Fig. 16), part of the equipment of a Viking ship, excavated from near London Bridge. Only in A.D. 1016, when the whole of England north of the Thames acknowledged the Danish Cnut (Canute) as king, was London forced to yield. Cnut established his court at Westminster, on Thorney Island, where Edward the Confessor was later to build his great abbey, and though London must still have been a town of simple timber-framed huts constantly imperilled by fire (St. Paul's burnt down in A.D. 961 and again in 1087), by the 11th century it was recognised as the foremost city in the land.

14 6th-century gilt-bronze brooch from the Saxon cemetery at Mitcham, Surrey.

12

15 Silver penny of Alfred, minted in London. On
the reverse is *LONDONIA* in monogram.

16 Viking battle-axe, perhaps lost in an attack on
London Bridge, *c.* 1000.

B

Medieval

The Normans were kinsfolk of the Vikings and Danes, and their occupation of 1066 may be regarded as just another in that long series of invasions to which Britain had been subject for many thousands of years, but with increasing ferocity since the 9th century. As it chanced, no subsequent successful invading army has ever yet crossed the Channel; but William the Conqueror was exceedingly conscious of the weakness of his position, and of the need both to placate and to overawe the population of London. His first acts were thus on the one hand, to guarantee the existing rights and privileges of its citizens, and, on the other, to build a fortress overshadowing the city (this he later reconstructed, and his mighty White Tower is the nucleus of the present Tower of London). The Normans continued to develop the Danish palace of Westminster, and William Rufus's magnificent Westminster Hall still survives to remind us of this. Along the river-side between Westminster and the port of London stood the mansions of the Norman magnates. Many of London's wealthier citizens also had fine stone houses, and the financial and political assistance which the citizens were able to offer the Crown in times of trouble (London came to wield more real political power in the Middle Ages than at any other time in its history) was bartered for increasing civic autonomy: Henry I conceded the right of appointing the sheriff (responsible for tax collection) and John the right to elect a Mayor.

Education and the care of the sick were in the hands of the Church, and its charity work is illustrated in the Museum by a 15th-century wrought-iron almsbox. There were over a hundred parish churches, and the first of the monasteries, that of St. Martin-le-Grand, was founded in 1068. The religious foundations owned large estates, and London in Norman times was still far from being totally developed.

17 Medieval iron spearhead with leaf-shaped blade, found in the City.

18 Mid-14th century iron sword, found in the river during the building of Westminster Bridge.

14

19 13th-century baluster-shaped pitcher splashed with green glaze.

20 Medieval plough-coulter of iron from the City Ditch, Aldersgate.

21 Model of Old St. Paul's, before the spire was destroyed by lightning in 1561.

22 Stone corbel from the Temple, Blackfriars.

It was possible for ordinary people living within the walls to have gardens and orchards, and, according to the account of William Fitz Stephen, the city was 'blest in the wholesomeness of its air.' Agriculture was carried on close to London, though probably not within its confines: the medieval plough-coulters in the Museum (Fig. 20) were excavated in Southwark and from the city ditch at Aldersgate. Even in such semi-rural conditions, however, riots and outbreaks of violence were as common as fires among the half-timbered houses, and the wearing of swords (Fig. 18) or daggers was a necessary precaution.

The heart of medieval London was in Cheap, a spacious market place surrounded by streets named after various commodities, Milk Street, Bread Street, the Poultry and so on, and from which narrow crowded lanes descended to the warehouses along the river. There stood the new bridge over the Thames, begun in 1176, the first stone bridge to be built anywhere in Europe since Roman times, and an immense source of pride to Londoners. Very soon, as London became more congested, following the rapid growth in its population during the 13th century, houses and shops began to encroach onto the bridge, and a model in the Museum shows Old London Bridge as it appeared by the beginning of the 17th century. The economic expansion of this period, and the problems to which it gave rise, are reflected in the spread of gilds, which were instituted to control conditions of employment and apprenticeship and the quality of goods produced.

Chaucer's London was a very different place from the Norman city described by Fitz Stephen. By 1381 there were three new parishes, the establishment of the Inns of Court in a belt north of the Temple was encouraging westerly growth (the pattern which fashionable development in London has consistently followed ever since), and the ward of Farringdon Without was created to administer these new western suburbs; poorer people were settling in Portsoken or Bishopsgate, and this tendency marked the beginnings of an 'east end'. As tenements began to multiply and upper storeys were added to houses, causing them to jut out over

23 14th-century lanterns of copper alloy from Smithfield.

24 Mid-15th century leather shoe with elongated toe.

25 14th-century bronze tripod cooking pot found under a house-floor in Blackfriars.

the narrow streets and alleys, the lack of
sanitation fostered disease and plague, and
during the course of the Black Death in the
mid-14th century, over a third of the
population perished. Late medieval London,
whose prosperity and dominating position
among English towns of this period was
founded on its quasi-monopoly of the wool
trade, was a place of much sharper contrasts
between enormous wealth and depths of
poverty than had been the case hitherto, and
it was the wealthy businessmen who ruled the
city through the power of the more important
of the gilds, notably the twelve great Livery
Companies: Guildhall, which was built in the
early 15th century, was the splendid symbol
of this merchant power.

26 Late 15th-century bronze seal of the Convent of
St. Mary, found in Newgate.

Very little of the sumptuous plate produced by
the goldsmiths of Cheapside for these
merchant princes has come down to us, and
for much of our knowledge of the costume,
property and everyday life of medieval
Londoners of all classes we are dependent on
the evidence of illuminated manuscripts,
stained glass, monumental brasses and literary
sources. Nonetheless, a great deal of valuable
material has been excavated, much of which is
informative about the lives of the less well-to-
do, and the Museum is especially rich in
pottery, including a fine series of glazed jugs
and pitchers (Fig. 19), some boldly decorated
in polychrome, others adorned with human
faces. Leatherware is well represented by
water-costrels, sheaths for daggers and groups
of shoes (Fig. 24); and metalwork by two
14th-century lanterns found in Smithfield
(Fig. 23), spurs and stirrups, bronze cooking
pots (Fig. 25) and cauldrons, door-keys,
purse-frames, buckles, brooches and other
articles of domestic or personal use. Perhaps
the most absorbing of the smaller objects are
the leaden badges, of which the Museum has
an important collection (Fig. 28), brought back
by pilgrims from their devotional travels. All
this material is arranged to illustrate different
themes in medieval London life, while some
pieces of 15th-century furniture (Fig. 27) are
displayed in a specially designed interior
setting. The entrance to the medieval gallery
is suitably dominated by a view of the interior
of Old St. Paul's, enlarged from an engraving
by Hollar.

27 Oak food cupboard, c. 1500. The pierced holes
provided ventilation.

28 Leaden pilgrim badges found in London,
commemorating visits to Walsingham (the
Annunciation badge) and Canterbury (the ampulla
of St. Thomas).

Tudor

Probably the most striking change in the physical appearance of London between the time of Chaucer and that of Shakespeare was caused by the dissolution of the monasteries in Henry VIII's reign, as these religious foundations still owned a high proportion of city land. Some of the monasteries eventually became schools – Charterhouse is one example – but others were converted into tenements, for the major problem in Tudor London was housing. The combination of a decreasing demand for agricultural labour as the result of the enclosure of land for sheep-farming and greatly enhanced opportunities in London, which was going through a boom period, meant that tens of thousands of newcomers flocked into the capital hoping to make their fortune. Their number was swollen in the reign of Elizabeth by Protestant refugees from northern Europe who settled in the nearby villages of St. Giles and St. Martin-in-the-Fields, establishing their own communities and churches there. Southwark, formerly a fashionable retreat, now became an overcrowded slum, the centre of London's more noisome industries, brewing and tanning, and a perpetual source of disorder. The notorious stews were situated there, and so were the bull and bear baiting pits, to be joined later by the Rose and the Globe, for the Elizabethan theatre was banned from the 'square mile'. In 1551 Southwark was incorporated as Bridge Ward Without.

The population of Roman London, even at the height of its prosperity, had probably never exceeded 20,000, and the figures were about the same for Norman London. At the end of the Middle Ages, this number had doubled to about 40,000, which was already three times as great as medieval Bristol or York, and comparable to the wealthy burgher cities of the Low Countries, Brussels, Bruges or Ghent. But by the close of Elizabeth's reign the

29 Late 15th-century majolica vase made in the Netherlands and found in King William Street.

30 Detail showing Bishopsgate, from a copper plate engraved with a section of the earliest map of London, c. 1558.

31 Norden's map of Westminster, 1593.

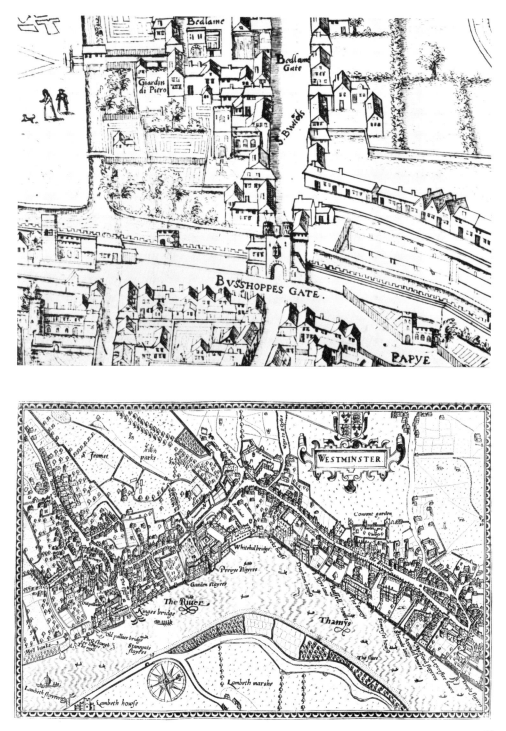

Bedlame

Bedlam Gate

Giardin di Piéro

J. Biwiek

BVSSHOPPES GATE.

PAPYE

Thames

parke

way to Sporte

WESTMINSTER

Covent garden

Whitehal bridge

Prevye stayres

Garden stayres

The River

Durham howse

Kinges bridge

Thames

ye O slawgh
ye hathe mill

Old pallaet bridge

Stanegate
stayres

Lambeth marshe

The stare

Moll banke

Lambeth stayres

Lambeth howse

21

population had risen to the staggering total of 200,000. Most people had to live beyond the walls, and since many of these areas lay outside the jurisdiction of the City and the gilds – Southwark was the last new City ward to be created – the result was not only unprecedented exploitation and slum development but the effective decline as far as London was concerned of the whole medieval system of civic local government and paternal control of labour, production and services. Nothing was to replace it until the latter part of the nineteenth century.

A series of royal proclamations on London housing designed to deal with the problem of the 'sinfully-polluted suburbes' met with little success, for such laws were hard to enforce, and the overcrowding and insanitary conditions were the direct cause of the increasingly severe attacks of plague which culminated in the appalling visitation of 1665, the Great Plague which started in the slums of St Giles-in-the-Fields, when 100,000 Londoners died (Fig. 46). But, as one of the two surviving sections of the earliest map of London shows (Fig. 30), there were still gardens and open fields close to the City walls at the beginning of Elizabeth's reign, while, along the Strand (Fig. 31), the great mansions of the nobility stretched down to the riverfront – Old Somerset House had been built in the 1540's by the Lord Protector, and Northumberland House, erected at the turn of the century, still survived at Charing Cross as recently as a hundred years ago. Parts of the Tudor palace of Whitehall can be studied in the drawing by Danckerts now in the Museum (Fig. 69).

The extravagance of Elizabethan architecture reflected not only the wealth, but the aspirations and enterprise, of its builders. This was the age when English seamen circumnavigated the globe, when the first joint-stock companies were started – the great East India Company was founded in 1600 – and when London replaced Antwerp as the financial centre of Europe, a position it still holds. The symbol of London's financial and commercial prosperity in the new age was the Royal Exchange, built by Sir Thomas Gresham, economic adviser to the Crown, in the heart of the City, between Cornhill and

32 Tilting helmet of russet steel made at the Greenwich armouries, c. 1540.

33 Woollen hat with ear flaps as worn by Tudor apprentices.

34 The Parr Pot, a white striped glass jug with London-made silver-gilt mounts, hallmarked 1546–7. Henry VIII had a large collection of ale-pots of this type.

35 Iron hook and weight from the steelyard perhaps given by Sir Thomas Gresham to the Royal Exchange in 1571.

36 Majolica plate, with a view of London and an inscription in praise of Queen Elizabeth, dated 1600 and probably made in London.

Threadneedle Street. A fine steelyard in the Museum (Fig. 35) bears Gresham's arms and may have been presented by him to the Exchange.

Foreign traders had been given rights in London since the Norman period (Lombard Street was named after the Italian bankers) but it was symptomatic of an age when economics was closely allied to patriotic feeling that the Hanseatic merchants, who had occupied part of the riverfront near Dowgate, were now deprived of their special privileges, and that many products, formerly imported from abroad, were imitated by London makers. Arms and armour of distinguished workmanship were made in the Royal Armoury at Greenwich (Fig. 32). Delft or majolica from the Netherlands was now imitated in Aldgate (Fig. 36). Venetian glass was made at Crutched Friars. Fine goldsmiths' work and jewellery had, of course, long been the pride of London: the superb silver-gilt mounts to the Parr Pot (Fig. 34) represent Tudor court taste, and the Cheapside Hoard, the stock-in-trade of a Jacobean jeweller, includes splendid examples of the delicate chains of gold, jewels and enamel (Fig. 38) which people in the 16th century loved to wear. The Museum's costume collection, one of the most extensive in Britain, includes examples not only of fashionable Elizabethan costume (Fig. 37), but of clothes worn by more ordinary people (Fig. 33), which rarely survives from any period: woollen hats, socks and gloves have been found in Finsbury Fields, London's rubbish dump for many centuries, where the marshy soil proved an admirable preservative.

37 Man's lavishly embroidered velvet cloak, doublet and hose, c. 1580-90.

38 Bracelets and necklaces from the hoard of early Jacobean jewellery found in Cheapside.

Stuart

The attractive prospect of London from Greenwich by an unknown Flemish artist (Fig. 41), which is the earliest painted view of London known, shows the capital as still quite a small town in the early 17th century, in spite of the rapid growth in its population in the Tudor period. Districts such as Hackney or Chiswick, now part of the inner suburbs, were then outlying villages noted for their healthful air or peaceful riverside setting: the Museum possesses an early Tudor wall-painting from Brooke House, Hackney, the retreat of a Dean of St. Paul's, and an important late 17th-century painting of Chiswick showing Old Corney House, with its garden and gazebo, and the cluster of Tudor houses round the church.

39 Oak four-poster bed, *c.* 1615, with mid-17th century embroidered hangings.

40 Brass lantern clock made by William Bowyer, *c.* 1650–60.

In the centre of London the innovation most significant for the future was the development of Covent Garden in the 1630's as a spacious square of uniform brick-built houses for upper-class residents. The controlling architect was Inigo Jones, whose church for the square can be seen in Hollar's engraving (Fig. 42). A similar development was in progress in Lincoln's Inn Fields at the outbreak of the Civil War. London remained staunch to the Parliamentary cause and an elaborate network of forts and trenches was constructed when the Royalists threatened the city. The citizens suffered much privation and loss of trade during the Rebellion and its aftermath, but the worst disaster to affect the capital in this or any other epoch of its long history was the Great Fire of 1666 (Fig. 45).

The rebuilding followed the old street pattern but new regulations about the heights of houses and the nature and quality of building materials were strictly enforced. The greatest legacy of the post-Fire period was undoubtedly the architecture of Sir Christopher Wren: the mighty dome of the new St. Paul's and the

41 Detail from a view of London from Greenwich, *c.* 1620–30, looking across the river and open fields to Southwark, with St. Paul's in the distance.

42 Covent Garden, *c.* 1640, an etching by Wenceslaus Hollar.

spires of his City churches have dominated the London skyline until our own day. But, in spite of a rapid recovery, the inclination for people of all classes, merchants and tradespeople as well as the rich, to move westwards away from the City accelerated after the Fire: Nicholas Barbon's speculative developments on the sites of the former mansions along the Strand, and the growth of the West End round the new court suburb of St. James's, reflected this tendency. To the east of the City, Spitalfields was occupied by French Huguenot refugees, who started the highly successful silk industry (Fig. 50), and the development of Stepney and neighbouring areas followed the rapid expansion of the port of London in the late 17th-century: the Howland Wet Dock, the first of its kind, was constructed in 1696.

London now supplied the whole country with manufactures, and many specialised industries grew up. Precision instruments are represented in the Museum by an early slide-rule, dated 1626, a surveying instrument made in 1658 and an important collection of clocks (Fig. 40) and watches. Of particular rarity are the fine silver-mounted trumpets by Augustine Dudley. Pottery from the different London workshops is abundant, and includes fine delftware (Fig. 43) as well as stoneware 'bellarmines' or beer containers for everyday use produced at Fulham by John Dwight. Among new London crafts coach-building may be mentioned – though the Museum has only a late 17th-century travelling trunk and sedan chair – but roads were still poorly constructed and maintained and London's principal highway remained the Thames. Hondius's painting of the great freeze of the Thames in 1676-7, and the picture of the Frost Fair held on the ice in 1683-4, are reminders that, even in the age of the coffee-house and of fashionable promenades like the Mall in St. James's Park, London life continued to centre on its river. At the end of the century, the population stood at close on 700,000.

43 London-made delft plate, the shape imitating a contemporary silver design.

44 Buff coat, c. 1620-30, the sleeves trimmed with braid.

45 Detail from a contemporary painting of the Great Fire, showing Old St. Paul's burning. The Fire raged unchecked for four whole days and devastated four-fifths of the city within the walls.

46 Scenes from a contemporary broadsheet illustrating the grim progress of the Plague.

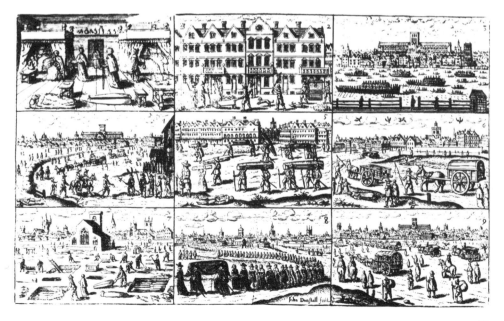

Georgian

47 An 18th-century chimney sweep. Watercolour by Paul Sandby, 1759.

The 18th century in England was an age of imperial expansion, growing overseas trade and enormously increased wealth, stimulating the luxury trades of the capital: and the Museum has a fine representative collection of Bow and Chelsea porcelain (Fig. 51). West End development took the form of growth round great squares: the streets were laid out with fine but standardised brick houses, and, in default of properly organised public utilities (the unit of local government was the parish, and the authority the usually inefficient parish vestry) the responsibility for paving, lighting and scavenging was entrusted to square trustees. By the end of the century, Oxford Street had become the finest of London's shopping streets, replacing Cheapside and to a certain extent the Strand. St James's became the *milieu* for clubs, and the most fashionable pleasure gardens, Vauxhall (Fig. 54) and Ranelagh, were laid out on the riverside beyond the built-up area. Further west, and stretching as far as Twickenham and Richmond, were the Thames-side retreats of the well-to-do: most of these pleasant villas, like Garrick's at Hampton, have now disappeared, but Marble Hill House, Twickenham, which was built for George II's mistress, survives in the care of the G.L.C. and can be visited.

Poverty, disease and the consumption of cheap spirits were between them, responsible for a high death rate in the first half of the century; and the widespread crime and more occasional but often serious outbreaks of mob violence, as in the Gordon Riots, were difficult to check. To meet this situation, hospitals, dispensaries and asylums were founded, all by private benefaction; and Fielding started the Bow Street runners or thief-takers, the precursors of the Metropolitan police, to supplement the aged watchmen with their wooden rattles (Fig. 52), who were all that the parish authorities

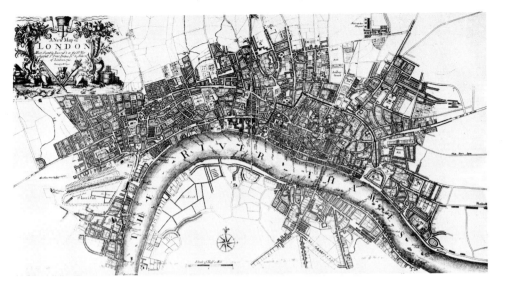

48 Parker's map of London in 1720, showing the
dramatic westward growth of the city.

49 Detail of the Park Lane area from Rocque's map
of London, 1746. The area north of Tyburn was not
developed until after 1760.

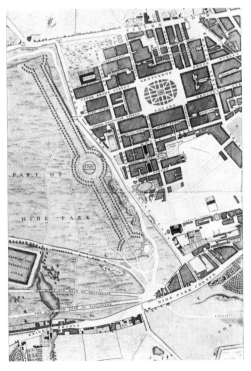

50 18th-century silk-warping mill used in Spitalfields.

51 'Winter', from a set of Seasons in Bow porcelain.

52 Wooden watchman's rattle, precursor of the police whistle.

provided. Fire services were organised by the different insurance companies, and the Museum has a good series of the company firemarks which were placed on houses eligible for protection, as well as a group of early fire engines.

Watermen operated ferries across the Thames, and (as illustrated in a painting in the Museum) coaches could be taken across on the horse-ferry between Millbank and Lambeth. But a new bridge at Westminster was opened to traffic in 1750, and Blackfriars followed in 1769. Roads were built across the Lambeth marshes, joining up at St. George's Circus, and the development of South London was at last a possibility. Roads were normally constructed now by turnpike trusts, who exacted a toll for their use, and it was this improvement that made possible the high-speed mail coaches and the faster communications of the Regency period. A number of early 19th-century carriages and other vehicles are in the Museum's collections. Canals (Fig. 55) made easier the transport of heavy goods, but the most urgent need at the turn of the century was the regeneration of the port, which lacked the facilities to handle the vast quantity of merchandise passing through the Pool of London. Without the magnificent series of docks on which construction started soon after 1800, London would have lost its commercial supremacy. Its prosperity depended, however, on the cheap labour which flooded into London, as into other towns, as the result of the decline in agriculture and its supersession by a manufacturing economy. London's population doubled from under a million to nearly two millions between 1801 and 1841, and about a third of the newcomers settled in the East End, creating in the process a belt of the most hideous slums that London had ever seen, stretching from Finsbury in the north to Bermondsey in the south.

C

53 Man's suit of figured silk, *c.* 1730-40.

54 One of the walks in Vauxhall Gardens, from an engraving of 1754. The statue of Handel is now in the Victoria and Albert Museum.

55 The entrance to the Regent's Canal at Limehouse. Watercolour by T. H. Shepherd, 1825.

56 Aquatint showing Nash's Regent Street Quadrant, 1822.

Victorian and Twentieth Century

In the course of the 19th century, when the British Empire spread all over the globe and ship-building was London's major industry, the volume of trade handled by the port of London multiplied by ten times, resulting in another vast increase in population. There were nearly two million inhabitants in London at the beginning of Queen Victoria's reign; at the end of it, there were about six and a half. The proportional increase was similar to those of the Tudor and Stuart periods; but the difference in the Victorian era was that, for the very first time, the metropolis grew dramatically in size, engulfing all the villages in the environs, until then still rural, and extending as far as Ealing in the west, Ilford and Greenwich in the east, Tottenham in the north, and Croydon in the south. The Museum's collection of 19th-century maps demonstrates the process in detail. This mushroom growth would not have been possible without entirely new forms of transport, and modern London was the product of the railway (Fig. 58). Euston, which connected London with Birmingham, was the first great station to be built, in 1837, and by the 1860's inner London was ringed with termini, while the new suburbs grew up round the stations along the railways. Buses, which had been introduced in 1829, catered principally for shorter journeys, but the increasing congestion (Fig. 64) in the streets of central London (a perennial problem) enforced major street improvements, such as the construction of the Embankment (Fig. 59), and resulted in the development of the world's first underground railway, the Metropolitan, opened in 1863.

Slums and public health were even more pressing a problem than congestion. The notorious rookeries of St. Giles and Saffron Hill were cleared, and the process of slum clearance was usually combined with street

57 The Long-Song Seller, one of the street traders interviewed by Henry Mayhew.

58 Building the Greenwich Railway. Detail from a watercolour by R. B. Schnebbelie, 1836.

59 The Victoria Embankment under construction. Watercolour by E. A. Goodall, 1865.

improvement, as in the case of Victoria Street, which was driven through the poorer parts of Westminster. Housing schemes like the Peabody estates were started through the generosity of private philanthropists, but private funds were insufficient to deal with every malady, and in 1856 the Metropolitan Board of Works, the precursor of the L.C.C., was brought into being, mainly to cope with the problem of sewage. Local government reform, long overdue, instituted County Councils in 1888, and the London boroughs were created eleven years later. In the fields of slum clearance, housing, education and the provision of open spaces for recreation, the L.C.C. accomplished miracles in a short space of time; and London was now becoming the focus for challenges to the Victorian economic system, exemplified by the Great Dock Strike of 1889 and the growth of the Labour movement.

Between the wars, the arterial roads brought light industry into the capital, the underground induced further outward sprawl, and the built-up area doubled, far outstripping the L.C.C. boundaries. Since 1945 the most significant factors in the development of London have been, first, the fine new local authority schools and housing estates, and the regeneration of the South Bank; then, the further rationalisation of local government through the creation of the G.L.C. in 1963; the drastic remodelling of the road system; the proliferation of high-rise buildings – flats, offices and hotels – so that London has become a skyscraper city in the space of 15 years; the complete renovation of large areas of central London, and the increasingly rapid disappearance of familiar landmarks and traditional employments. In an age when the whole port of London and life of the river can vanish almost overnight as the result of improved technology, and not only the appearance but the atmosphere of London is changing at a faster rate than ever before, when the standards of work and quality of output that have been the admiration of foreigners since the Middle Ages are in tragic and seemingly irreversible decline, the Museum's responsibilities as the guardian of the past and passing have become correspondingly greater and its task more urgent.

60 Cream silk wedding dress worn by Queen Mary, 1893.

61 Telephone, *c.* 1895.

62 Suffragette poster, 1910.

63 A street scene in Belsize Park, 1917. Oil painting
by Robert Bevan.

64 Scene at the Bank intersection, showing a
hansom cab and early types of 'bus. Drawing by
George Chambers, *c.* 1865.

Some of the architectural and social changes that took place in the course of the Victorian age are illustrated in paintings or drawings in the Museum: O'Connor's view of Pentonville Road, with trams passing and St. Pancras in the background, or Bevan's suggestion of the stuccoed Italianate streets characteristic of certain of the inner suburbs (Fig. 63), are cases in point. But the nature of the urban sprawl or of solutions to this problem like Hampstead Garden Suburb, and the character of later 19th and 20th century London life generally, are better and more fully recorded in photographs, which the Museum is now beginning to collect systematically. Furniture, pottery, textiles and domestic articles of all kinds, including an ornate piano shown at the Great Exhibition of 1851, illustrate the often claustrophobic nature of the Victorian interior. Two early bicycles are reminders of the Victorians at leisure, and examples of early typewriters and telephones (Fig. 61) demonstrate the increasing importance of mechanical appliances in daily life. The changing rôle of women in early 20th-century life is illustrated by the activities of the Suffragettes (Fig. 62), whose records and personalia were presented to the Museum by the Suffragette Fellowship. The lack of 20th-century material of other types – even the costume collection is weaker in its coverage of the present century – will, it is hoped, be remedied shortly. The work of a museum like our own cannot be brought to a convenient halt at a point some hundred or more years ago when that particular moment in time has started to come into historical focus and the collecting of its material remains is already a reputable activity. History begins with yesterday.

65 Christ Church, Newgate Street, after its destruction by incendiary bombs in 1941. Oil painting by John Piper.

66 Construction of the Underpass at Hyde Park Corner, 1961. Oil painting by Bernard Dunstan.

Special
Rooms

Shop Fronts

67 Georgian shop-fronts as reconstructed. The ironmonger's stood in High Holborn, the stationer's in Greenwich and the milliner's in Brentford.

Glass

Though the London Museum was founded, in friendly rivalry to the Musée Carnavalet in Paris, to illustrate the archaeology, history and social life of the metropolis, and the collections have been brought together for their historical importance in this context rather than for any specialist or aesthetic significance they might possess, it would be greatly the poorer without a number of special collections which have accrued as a result of the generosity of benefactors who have taken a particular interest in the Museum.

One of the most important of such benefactions is the collection of English table glass, amongst the finest ever assembled, formed at the end of his life by Sir Richard Garton (1857–1934); this was lent to the Museum at his death, and subsequently, in 1943, generously presented by his heirs. The 437 pieces in the collection range in date from the mid-17th century to the beginning of the 19th, and, though largely composed of goblets and wine-glasses (Fig. 68), also include bowls, candlesticks, decanters, jelly-glasses and sweetmeat baskets. The earliest and most important specimen is the Chesterfield Flute, the only example of English make to come down to us of this type of mid-17th century glass. There is a 'crisselled' or clouded bowl dating from before the perfection of Ravenscroft's 'lead crystal' process in 1676, and some fine late 17th-century pieces, including a punch bowl, two decanter-jugs and two giant ceremonial goblets, all 'à la facon de Venise'. In addition, the collection is remarkable for its representation of the full range of designs and decorative motifs used in glass-making during the 18th century. With some rare exceptions, no two pieces are exactly alike.

68 Mid-18th century Jacobite glass, from the Garton Collection.

Prints and Drawings

The Museum's Print Room contains about 3,000 watercolours and drawings and about 7,000 prints, illustrative of the topography or social life of London from the 17th century to the present day. It is anticipated that, in the course of time, the collection of photographs will be the principal source of record for the period from the second half of the 19th century onwards. Thematic exhibitions comprising 50 or 60 prints and drawings are arranged at intervals.

The earliest important topographical drawing is the Danckerts view of Whitehall and Westminster from across St. James's Park, executed about 1675 (Fig. 69). Twelve of Sandby's series of watercolours of the cries of London (Fig. 47), some of which were engraved in 1760, are in the collection, and among the 40-odd watercolours and drawings by Rowlandson, the most noteworthy are the *Skaters on the Serpentine* and the scene of people enjoying themselves at one of the pleasure gardens (Fig. 70). Among the most accurate and attractive topographical views are those of R. B. Schnebbelie (Fig. 58) and T. H. Shepherd (Fig. 55), the latter of whom was particularly concerned in his later years with recording streets and buildings due for demolition. Philip Norman is well represented with drawings of a similar intent; and there is a large collection of pencil sketches of blitzed buildings by Joseph Bato. Examples of humorous drawings range from Rowlandson to Fougasse, and include an impression of a London fog, once in the possession of Charles Dickens. Among the prints may be mentioned etchings by Hollar (Fig. 42) and Whistler and fine aquatints such as the series of London turnpikes, Daniell's views of the docks, and Pollard's coaching inns.

69 Detail from a drawing by Hendrick Danckerts, *c.* 1675, showing the Banqueting House and Cockpit of Whitehall Palace.

70 Taking tea at the White Conduit House. Watercolour by Thomas Rowlandson, 1787.

44

The Stage

The collection of material relating to the London stage is mainly composed of costume and accessories, and includes items on permanent loan from the Royal Shakespeare Theatre. Noteworthy among the theatre costumes are those worn by Edmund Kean as Richard III, Irving as Malvolio and King Lear, Fred Terry as the Scarlet Pimpernel, and Ivor Novello in *The King's Rhapsody*. Irving's wardrobe is especially well represented. Among relics of the operatic stage are a collection of stage jewellery and other accessories used by Adelina Patti, and her costume as Rosina in *The Barber of Seville*. Ballet is represented by an extensive collection of costumes and accessories worn by Anna Pavlova, among them the dress she wore in *The Dying Swan*, and by costumes designed for the Diaghilev Ballet, including the magnificent robes for the Countess and the Fairy Carabosse from his production of *The Sleeping Princess* at the Coliseum, 1921. The development of the circus, music-hall and variety stage is also illustrated and exhibits include the costume worn by the famous early 19th-century clown Grimaldi (Fig. 71), the suit used by George Robey, and Psycho, Maskelyne's original whist-playing automaton. Of the theatrical pictures in the Museum the Hayman of Garrick and Mrs. Pritchard, the portraits of Irving and Walter Lambert's canvas *Popularity*, portraits of the stars of the Edwardian music-hall stage, may be singled out as of special interest. The collections also include Garrick's death mask, the piano used by W. S. Gilbert, a Dulac figure of Sir Thomas Beecham conducting, tinsel pictures, playbills and programmes.

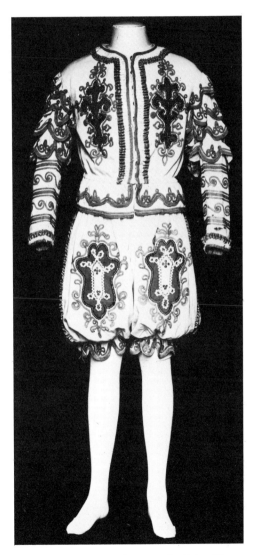

71 Clown's costume, *c.* 1805, worn by Grimaldi.

45

Toys and Games

The London Museum has always extended a special welcome to children, and its schools service has been one of the pioneers in this sphere of museum educational activity. It is appropriate, therefore, that from the beginning it should have collected examples of children's toys and games. The most comprehensive collection is that of dolls, of which the most important and interesting are Queen Victoria's (Fig. 72). The dolls' houses include a fine early 18th-century example, completely furnished (Fig. 73). Another major constituent is the collection of 19th-century toy theatre sets, part of the Jonathan King Collection (which also includes an unrivalled series of Valentine cards): these sets consist of sheets of characters and scenes, originally sold for a penny plain or twopence hand-coloured, which were intended to be cut out and inserted into slides that could be pushed on and off a model stage. There is an extensive series of table games, notably jig-saw puzzles, which were devised for instructional purposes as well as for amusement; and a large collection of penny toys, tiny models in painted tin of vehicles, animals and other objects which were made in Germany (the leading toy manufacturing country until 1914) at the beginning of the century and sold by street hawkers on Ludgate Hill and in Cheapside. Noteworthy among other toys are a 17th-century rocking horse, a wooden train dating from the earliest days of the railway, a mid 19th-century Noah's Ark, late 19th-century tops and yo-yos, an early clockwork tricycle, and a wooden open-topped London 'bus dating from 1925.

72 Dolls from a collection of 132 dressed by Queen Victoria as a girl.

73 Doll's house, c. 1740, with contemporary wallpaper and furniture.

Royal Costume

From its inception in 1911 the London
Museum has been helped most generously by
successive generations of the Royal Family,
and many of the most spectacular exhibits,
notably the robes worn at the Coronations of
1838 (Fig. 74), 1902, 1911 and 1937, are royal
gifts or loans. This is fitting, since London has
been the home of the Sovereign and the centre
of national government since Saxon times, and
the London Museum is rightly more than just
a local museum: it should be able to illustrate
royal and national ceremonial, to provide a
pageant of British social history and to mirror
the whole political and economic life of the
nation.

The earliest royal costumes are those belonging
to Charles I, clothes and boots worn in
childhood, and the blue silk vest he wore at his
execution in 1649. More comprehensive is the
collection of dresses worn by Queen Victoria:
these include her wedding-dress and a dress
of black silk dating from 1894 which gives us
a vivid impression of the Queen in old age. The
Museum also contains the wedding-dresses of
Princess Charlotte (daughter of George IV),
Queen Mary, and H.R.H. The Princess
Margaret, Countess of Snowdon, whose simple
but beautiful gown in white silk organza was
designed by Norman Hartnell. Amongst other
exhibits are the model of the state coach built
about 1760, with side panels painted by
Cipriani, a number of crown frames, a cradle
and swing-cot used for Queen Victoria's
children, and a large painting of the
Coronation procession of 1937 passing down
Piccadilly by Sir John Lavery.

74 Coronation robes of scarlet velvet trimmed and
lined with ermine, worn by Queen Victoria.

How to reach the London Museum

By underground to Queensway (Central Line), High Street Kensington or Bayswater (Circle and District Lines)

By bus to Queensway (12,88), Palace Gate (9,33,49,52,73) or Church Street (27,28,31,52)

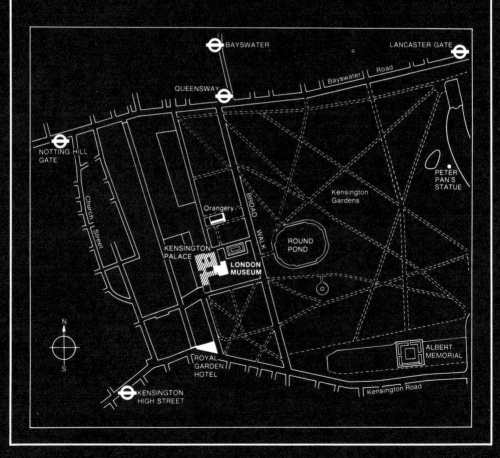